Towards the Conversion of England

A Report Revisited

Geoff Pearson
Vicar of St Bartholomew, Roby
Area Dean of Huyton

GROVE BOOKS LIMITED
RIDLEY HALL RD CAMBRIDGE CB3 9HU

Contents

Church Army supports the Grove Evangelism Series

Church Army is a society of evangelists within the Anglican Communion that trains, supports and deploys evangelists across the UK and Ireland to enable people to come to a living faith in Jesus Christ.

Church Army—sharing faith through words and action

For more information about Church Army go to www.churcharmy.org.uk or phone 0208 309 3519 or email info@churcharmy.org.uk

Church Army, Marlowe House, 109 Station Rd, Sidcup, Kent DA15 7AD
Registered Charity number: 226226

The Cover Illustration is by Peter Ashton

First Impression August 2005
ISSN 1367-0840
ISBN 1 85174 599 8

Introduction 1

This is not an in-depth study of a long-forgotten report, but a personal reflection of a significant document which excites me because, on its 60ᵗʰ anniversary, it still seems relevant today. The context has changed but the content of the gospel has not.

Indeed, *Towards the Conversion of England* (TTCE)[1] is even more relevant now as our country is more post-Christian than it was in 1945. In consequence, I have tried to connect the far-reaching proposals made then with the opportunities and possibilities we have now.

Although an Anglican paper, I hope you see the relevance in other churches too. I have used the same chapter headings and the quotations from Archbishop William Temple which opened each chapter of the report as the framework, referring to page numbers in TTCE for quotations as we go along. Sadly the original report is no longer available, not even as a web resource, so quotations are given.

The original report was compiled by 50 members. It was so popular that it had run through five further printings by November 1945. It encouraged clergy to learn how to share their faith and stressed the importance of an active and mobilized laity. It was pioneering in its emphasis on cells and the possibilities of advertising. The appointment of diocesan missioners can be traced to this publication.

If only the follow-up had not been undermined by the post-war rebuilding of churches and a decision to revise canon law.

Both the report and this booklet offer suggestions as to how we can address that decline and declare the name of Jesus

TTCE begins with an analysis of decline, but read on! Both TTCE and this booklet offer suggestions as to how we can address that decline and declare the name of Jesus. There are signs of hope and opportunities to be taken.

TTCE spoke of 'broad brush strokes,' which is what I also offer here.

2 The Situation Before the Church

> We must still claim that Christianity enables us to 'make sense' of the world, not meaning that we can show that it is sense, but with a more liberal and radical meaning of making sense of what, till it was transformed, is largely nonsense — a disordered chaos waiting to be reduced to order as the Spirit of God gives it shape. Our problem is to envisage the task of the church to a largely alien world.   William Temple

The Church of England report 60 years ago described the 'drift from organized religion,' the 'decline of church-going' and the 'collapse of Christian moral standards' (TTCE, pp 2, 3, 4). It was also acknowledged then that 'pulpit preaching can no longer be relied on as the principle medium for evangelization'!

More recently the Chief Rabbi, Jonathan Sachs, wrote:

> Today it would be fair to say that Christianity finds itself for the first time in a situation familiar to the Jews for 2,000 years — the condition of being a minority in the world whose values we do not entirely share.[2]

We are even more in the minority than we were in 1945, but can note that we have been there before, in pre-Christendom days. Lesslie Newbigin observes a difference however:

> It is a pagan society, and its paganism, having been born out of rejection of Christianity, is far more resistant to the gospel than the pre-Christian paganism with which cross-cultural missions have been familiar.[3]

> Christianity's new position today is as one voice among many.

> National Decline in Churchgoing

As this TTCE heading notes, decline has been with us a long time in the Church of England. Figures first published in *The UK Christian Handbook: Religious Trends* show that, at the current rate, total church membership across Britain will have fallen to 5,598,000 by the end of 2005, down by more than a million people in 15 years. Projections for the Church of England have shown that, based on percentage decline as in the 1990s, we can expect an adult attendance figure in 2030 of about 500,000 and the child attendance would fall to almost nothing.[4]

The Collapse of Christian Moral Standards

TTCE (p 4) states in the context of the Second World War, 'that there is so little feeling of shame in loose living, still less in untruthfulness or dishonesty.' My view is that 60 years later we are a country whose standards have been lowered further and whose sensitivities have been blunted. The fear of God has diminished in that time, and, if you lack the fear of God, then you are not so worried about sin. Note, even in 1945 it was observed 'there is today little consciousness of sin'! TTCE (p 25).

The latest government figures conservatively suggest that 300,000 children have addict parents published 2003

My newspaper today contains alarming statistics about addiction and the binge-drinking culture that is causing problems in town centres, as well as an article on drug abusers who neglect and maltreat their children. The latest government figures conservatively suggest that 300,000 children have addict parents. Frank Field MP published *Neighbours From Hell: The Politics of Behaviour* in which he suggests that we are reaping a whirlwind of bad behaviour due to our failure to consider the most basic of political questions: 'What kind of character do we want our fellow citizens to have?'[5]

TTCE (p 6) refers to 'the age-long lie' of humanism, and re-affirms the need to consider sin in relation to God. This is not popular theology today and in my view does need re-affirming. I am reminded of the great Victorian writer and thinker, George MacDonald, who insisted that both individuals and nations are on spiritual journeys of either becoming better or worse. In *Princess and Curdie* he writes: 'All men, if they do not care, go down hill to the animals' country… many men are actually, all their lives, going to be beasts.'[6]

Death of Christian Britain

Callum Brown has argued cogently that the nation's core religious culture has been destroyed.[7] He makes a powerful challenge to the view that secularization has been a long and gradual process and argues that there was a catastrophic and abrupt cultural revolution in the 1960s. Penny Thompson in her book, *Whatever Happened to Religious Education?* charts the trend of teachers not to approach RE from a committed Christian view of the world.[8] It was also in the mid-60s that John Lennon said 'Christianity will go, it will vanish and shrink,

I needn't argue about that. I'm right and I will be proved right. We're more popular than Jesus now.'[9] Note too, that this was also a time of theological radicalism when we recall the *Honest to God* debate and the uncertain note sounded by the church.

Could things crumble so quickly? Is Callum Brown right? As I reflected on this, I was surprised to think how quickly individual churches can both rise and decline. Most of all I am aware how easy it is for hearts to grow cold and hard. This can happen in a short period of time, so why not on a national scale too? Is it any wonder that, when Bishop Lesslie Newbigin returned from the mission field in India in the 1970s, his response to the situation in Britain was to point up 'the disappearance of hope.'[10]

Underlying Causes

TTCE (pp 10, 12) suggested the chief causes of decline were humanism and secular education. These forces have continued as the spiritual dimension has been further eroded.

Children's Agenda Still Not Properly Addressed

In 1992 the report *All God's Children* spoke of children's evangelism in crisis.[11] The report received much verbal support but its recommendations were far too modest and little action took place. In 1993 I published *Save Our Children*, in response, and pleaded for children to be on the church's agenda so that we rediscover true childlikeness and move away from an adult-centred church that excludes children by giving them little theological or pastoral significance.[12] Until we reverse this process, millions of children will face adult life without any awareness of a God who loves them.

Five years later, with Penny Frank, in *Too Little—Too Late! (Children's Evangelism Beyond Crisis)*, I expressed grief at having to report failure.[13] We called for some passion for a lost generation and more energy and resources to be given for any serious effort to evangelize the children of this nation. In 1999 I wrote (with Capt Philip Clark CA) *Kidz Klubs—The Alpha of Children's Evangelism*, in which we described a model of working with children that is proving a positive and effective means of communicating God's love and truth to children normally beyond the church's reach.[14]

So there is hope but, I would still argue, a long way to go

In 2001, the Church of England appointed an Archbishop's Officer for Evangelism among Children. She quickly set about a new Church of England children's strategy.[15] So there is hope but, I would still argue, a long way to go, as 'between one in 3 and one in 4 children disappeared from Sunday church between 1990 and 2000.'[16]

Power of the Media

The TTCE report (p 106) was prophetic about the immense influence of the cinema and the forthcoming television which 'might conceivably become the greatest single influence on the minds and lives of our people, exceeding the power of radio, film and the press.' Today the soaps act like drugs with the writers the pushers, skilfully sustaining the craving for more. In Liverpool, most of my funeral visits include the comment 'she preferred *Coronation Street* to *Eastenders*', or *vice versa*.

How do we respond to this now? One way is to take all the media opportunities which TTCE advocated, and then locally to take all the positive opportunities modern media affords. Resources here include two Grove books, *Faith and Film*[17] and *Using your Church Web Site for Evangelism*[18] as well as the Christian Enquiry Agency[19] and the ReJesus website,[20] both of which are available for all churches to use in their evangelism strategy.

Postmodernity

TTCE (p 6) refers to humanism as the 'age-long lie.' Now we might look further at the postmodern experience with its reaction against institutions, including organized religion.

Bel Mooney's book, *Devout Sceptics*, is a reminder that people have not ceased to search for God. However, their search for the numinous or some dimension of the spirit that transcends the mundane is not going to be restricted to what the church counts as orthodoxy.

> Devout sceptics are seekers who won't trust the maps they have been given, but know there is a destination towards which to stumble...[21]

The danger, of course, in this pick'n'mix process is that people are so questioning and so open minded to many truths that they never actually come down on any truth. And the truth can never be neutral. The intelligent sceptics who reckon that their searching leads them to an understanding of what it means to be human and a desire to be better are often too easily diverted.

Consumerism

I would also want to add 'consumerism' to the TTCE report, which was originally written on very cheap paper in a time of rationing.

Today there seems to be a buying tide that exalts individual choice and persuades people that top brands have some significance

Consumption defines the dominant relationship we have with the world rather than stewardship and care

for life. The free market ideology has taken over the pursuit of grander ideologies. And consumption defines the dominant relationship we have with the world rather than stewardship and care. 'Postmodernism is consumption,' says Alan Storkey, 'buying, advertisements, TV culture, in-your-face entertainment, shopping, pressure, thing-filled living.'[22] It is gaining the world and forfeiting your soul.

We have silenced the rumours of transcendance and ignored the mystery of wonder

And yet, it is existential despair that usually develops in a time of excess and plenty. It is the most technologically advanced countries that are marked by family breakdown, drug addiction, alcoholism, abortion, violent crime, homelessness and suicide. There is a human stain across our best efforts. We have silenced the rumours of transcendence and ignored the mystery of wonder. We have forgotten what it means to be poor in spirit and rich in faith.

Networks

The *Mission-shaped Church* report reminds us forcefully that community is increasingly being re-formed around networks, and that people are now less inclined to make lasting commitments.[23] In many ways the church has been slow to come to grips with this change whereby geography no longer seems to be the primary basis of community. Today, Fresh Expressions is one creative way in which we can connect the gospel to the new paradigm.[24]

The Gospel

> The gospel is true always and everywhere, or it is not a gospel at all, or true at all. **William Temple**

According to the TTCE Report 'The Eternal Gospel' is:

- The good news that God is, and that God is love.
- The good news that God has intervened and done for us what we could not do for ourselves.
- The good news that God was in Christ, reconciling the world to himself.
- The good news of the 'restoration of all things in Christ.'
- The good news that God in Christ has opened the kingdom of heaven to all believers.
- The good news of the new life to be enjoyed in the fellowship of Christ's church.
- The good news of the power of the Holy Spirit available to the members of Christ.
- The good news of redemption to eternal life.
- The good news of the final triumph of the good, and that Jesus has opened the way of escape from the power of sin, from the fear of judgment and from everlasting death.

If written today I would anticipate TTCE having more emphasis on creation and the Trinity, with more reference to the riches of the churches in this ecumenical era, but with less emphasis on fear, judgment and everlasting death. Would you agree?

It is easy to dismiss doctrine as too difficult, too obscure and as coming to us in credal statements that do not scratch where people itch. Why not plunge in straight away with ethical issues, which is where many young people are starting from, particularly thinking about the environment, suffering and injustice? Dr Donald English taught:

None of the great problems faced by the world will be solved except by reference to what God has revealed in Jesus Christ. His life and teaching, his death and resurrection, his ascension, and our hope of his second coming are directly related to starvation and ecology, to racism and deprivation, to war and injustice, to unemployment and genetic engineering. The link is not always obvious, and the biblical preacher will need to know about both subjects. The implication of Jesus as the word of creation is that what God has revealed through him provides us with the values by which to face the world's problems. People desperately need biblical preachers to make that clear.[25]

English himself demonstrated this approach, as TTCE would have advocated, especially on the radio programme *Thought For The Day*.

The Presentation of the Gospel

But how can we get a hearing for the great doctrines and wonderful gospel concepts? Is not the soil too mixed up with scientific knowledge, humanism, consumerism and hopelessness to receive the gospel seed?

We need to look again at the classic definition of evangelism given in TTCE (p 1) and then see how it applies.

To evangelize is so to present Christ Jesus in the power of the Holy Spirit, that men shall come to put their trust in God through him, to accept him as their saviour, and serve him as their king in the fellowship of his church.

On the one hand today we would want inclusive language, while on the other a less prescriptive outcome. Perhaps we would reflect more on the New Testament writers who often start in different places in telling the story, using different analogies to communicate the gospel to their particular audience, whilst aware of the understanding on which they draw.

Today we understand afresh that Jesus is the model for starting where people are, getting alongside them, affirming them, responding to their needs and questions, and challenging them, as he did with the couple on the Emmaus Road. He moved them on in their understanding, but did not pressurize them, or make them conform. They in turn used their freedom to invite him in.

Reflecting some of the recommendations from TTCE in today's context, below are some examples of how I think this can be done in practice.

Media

As already mentioned, TTCE had much to say about modern media being used for the gospel. Today TV and cinema are the modern sources of revelation, not of Christian doctrine, but about ourselves and our world, as well as the signs of the times.

> Film offers us a creative language, an imaginative language of movement and sound that can bridge the gap between the rational and the aesthetic, the sacred and the secular, the church and the world, and thereby open fresh new windows on a very old gospel.

So says Brian P Stone in *Fact and Film — Theological Themes at The Cinema*.[26] His book uses film themes illustrating each section of the Apostles' Creed for use in discussion groups. Other publications do the same with TV programmes, for example, the Scripture Union *Connect* studies on *Friends* and *The Simpsons*.

Apologetics

Many people have intellectual roadblocks, particularly students. Christian students are challenged more than ever to give account of the hope within them. I was particularly impressed by one student outreach I encountered where students negotiated with the manager of a coffee shop to stay open late. He was guaranteed custom and the students had the opportunity, with a relevant topic, to reply to questions. One group called this meeting a 'Hot Potato' night while another, which met in a pub, was called 'Pints of View.'

Christian students are challenged more than ever to give account of the hope within them

Process Evangelism

This is an awkward heading that reminds us that evangelism is a much longer process than we may have thought. John Finney in 1984 found that on average the time for most people to become Christian was four years.[27] TTCE (pp 130, 131) says 'the discussion group stands high among additional opportunities for training in the faith' while 'study cells belong to another and quite distinct movement…to exhibit the marks of a direct moving of the Holy Spirit.'

We know today of the cell church movement and the significant contribution that courses like *Alpha, Emmaus* and *Essence* have in our postmodern and even less cerebral context than 60 years ago. These and many other courses provide accessible points of entry, and contemporary culture in all its diversity needs opportunities for people to come to faith in more than one way.

Kidz Klub
TTCE (p 87) says 'it is impossible to exaggerate the importance of bringing children to a simple and definite trust in God.' A modern programme which has this conviction at its heart is Kidz Klub. This very fresh expression of church reaches children who are unaware of the Christian story—which is now most of them.

Developed in America by pioneer Bill Wilson, this loud, magazine-style programme is an attempt to respond to the culture of today without compromising God's values and the message of salvation. Yes, there are noisy games, but every week the teaching time contains a one-concept lesson, taken from the Bible, which is presented in a number of different ways. Alongside the teaching element there is a relational element through the weekly visits each child receives. It takes a lot of commitment, but this comes readily from those who know that reaching children is truly a matter of life and death.

The Seasons and a Twelve Month Liturgical Cycle
TTCE (p 82) speaks of the parish priest being 'the key to the evangelistic situation' and occasional offices (baptisms, confirmation, weddings and funerals, p 43) providing 'eminent opportunities for evangelism,' especially in a country parish. We find that true in our urban environment too and warm to this offering from our bishop to note that every month is marked by commercial opportunity, which is also a spiritual opportunity which we can use in special services.

January—New Year Resolutions—Repentance and New Promises

February—Valentine's Day—Celebration of Love

March—Mothering Sunday—Importance of Family Bonds

April—Easter—Forgiveness and Life after Death

May—Bank Holidays—Holiday; Times of Refreshment

June—Father's Day—Family and Roots

July/August—Summer Fairs—Community Solidarity

September—School Starts—Changes and New Beginnings

October—Harvest—Providence and Environment

November—Remembrance—Bereavement

December—Christmas—Peace on Earth

These and other examples are endeavouring to start where people are.

The Apostolate of the Whole Church 4

> The evangelization of England…is a work that cannot be done by the clergy alone; it can only be done to a very small extent by the clergy at all. There can be no widespread evangelization of England unless the work is undertaken by the lay people of the church…The main duty of the clergy must be to train the lay members of the congregation in their work of witness. William Temple

The Part of the Clergy in Evangelism

TTCE (pp 40, 41) says parish clergy need 'relief from heavy routine duty' and a new vision, fresh hope and a baptism of the Holy Spirit, for the evangelistic task. What still blocks this and what dampens rather than fans the flame of evangelism is often a busyness and a weariness in well-doing.

The top two pressures felt by clergy are the amount of internal administration and the amount of external bureaucracy.[28] Both relate to administration, which is something clergy feel is not central to their ministry and calling. It is frequently said that the clergy are trained for pastoral ministry rather than mission outreach, as noted in TTCE (p 60). Now I suggest that:

Clergy Identify Their Own Style of Evangelism
It takes all kinds of Christians to reach all kinds of non-Christians. Some operate around the confrontational style, some around the intellectual style, some around the testimonial style, some around the interpersonal style and some around the invitational style. For more detail, see the course *Becoming a Contagious Christian*, which is all about communicating your faith in a style that suits you.[29]

Parishes Appoint a Director of Evangelism…
…or equivalent, who will train the church in evangelism. Such a person will find and equip evangelists. He or she will develop diversified evangelism teams and develop a wide and diverse range of outreach ministries and events. If having such a person seems too ambitious for each parish then perhaps it could be a deanery appointment. The same training and equipping will need to happen with the Evangelism

13

Facilitator (or whatever title seems appropriate) persevering in raising evangelism values in all the other local churches in the area.

Clergy Aim to be Courageous Leaders

I have no doubt whatsoever that effective churches have in common the fact that they are led by people who possess and deploy the spiritual gift of leadership. They are leaders who have vision—defined as a picture of the future that produces passion. The omnicompetent vicar needs to give way to the visionary, bold, leader who can offer a step-by-step explanation of how to move from vision to reality. Such a leader will be able to say 'no' to work not in line with their vision. They will keep their passion hot by whatever means, not least study leave and energizing teamwork. As Bill Hybels says, 'The best gift I can give to the people I lead is a healthy, energized, fully surrendered and focused self.'[30]

Role of the Laity in Evangelism

TTCE (p 58): 'We are convinced that England will never be converted until the laity use the opportunities for evangelism daily afforded by their various professions, crafts and occupations.'

But do we encourage and train along these lines? When I travelled around the country with a mission brief, I was constantly struck by the relief experienced as a result of a simple explanation describing the difference between a witness and an evangelist—how we are all called to be witnesses but not all called to be evangelists. That special gift that enabled people to come right into the kingdom depended so much on a chain of witnesses who had helped people through various stages of belief to come to the point where they were ready to make that final, decisive step.

One challenge is to understand where people are in their faith journey so that we can help to communicate the gospel in relevant ways. Then there are plenty of courses to help train the laity in evangelism, such as, *Lost for Words*[31] and *Becoming a Contagious Christian*. From an Australian course *Gossiping the Gospel* I use there are some simple exercises to help people in their faith sharing.[32] We divide a group into threes. We remind people that to be a Christian is to be different and that they probably need good reason to stand against the pressure of unbelief and turning away from church. I then give each person strictly one minute to say to others, 'I am still a Christian because…' avoiding Christian jargon and speaking honestly from the heart.

Two groups then join together and each person is asked to tell the story in summary form of the one who was on their right in the group of three. ('*Name* is still a Christian because…') I then write up people's reasons under the title:

'Because.' When all have contributed, I change the title to something like, 'O Lord we know you are real because...' and then invite people to stand and read it together as a prayer-litany. This is often a powerful moment when people realize the greatness of God and the variety of ways in which he relates to people.

We discuss why we had only a minute to share and why listening was so important. I cannot remember a session when people have been stuck for words, and it is always good to affirm people for the confidence with which they spoke. They go away feeling that they have begun to share their faith effectively. *Through Faith Missions*[33] have given hundreds of people the above experience with their 'walks' in different parts of the country, and the material from *Imagine*[34] will help local people see how they can be a Christian witness at work.

My experience is that most people are too long in telling their story. They often need advice in getting rid of religious terminology and occasional weird supernatural stories. Help in telling their story humbly is always welcome as it avoids any tinge of superiority.

People, I contend, are happy to serve and ready to witness when they own a particular vision and when they pick up the urgency. Once they have experienced the thrill of seeing someone becoming a believer, a Christ-follower, helped by their witness, then usually they want more of the thrilling action. Michael Green notes about laypeople in the early church:

> They went everywhere spreading the good news, which had brought joy, release and a new life to themselves. This must often have been not formal preaching, but informal chattering to friends and chance acquaintances, in homes and in shops, on walks and around market stalls. They went everywhere *gossiping the gospel*; they did it naturally, enthusiastically, and with the conviction of those who are not paid to say that sort of thing. Consequently they were taken seriously, and the movement spread...[35]

In addition, TTCE pointed out that certain vocations offer peculiar opportunities for evangelism and are key posts to Christian influence. If we are operating from the margins, we may well have to target certain professions. Teachers are a key influence, as are those who work in the media. When people look back in life and consider their role-model, the person who helped them most through their spiritual journey, then it is often a teacher or a relation.

This does not take away from the constraint that all Christians are under to carry their faith and loyalty into concrete situations, the daily business and the personal relations of their life. According to TTCE, evangelism in the working world means claiming for Christ the whole of the particular occupation in which we are engaged, and the doing of our work to reflect his likeness.

5 Evangelism: Proclaiming the Gospel

> It is quite futile saying to people: 'Go to the Cross.' We must be able to say: 'Come to the Cross.' And there are only two voices which can issue that invitation with effect. One is the voice of the sinless Redeemer, with which we cannot speak; and one is the voice of the forgiven sinner, who knows himself forgiven, that is our part.   William Temple

The gospel needs to be proclaimed and presented in such a way that a definite decision of the will is called for. The definition of 'One beggar telling another beggar where to find bread' is helpful in dispersing any feeling of superiority.

The temptation in a situation where we are highlighting a process is that we can too easily resist the question, 'What would prevent you receiving Christ right now?' Praise God for the gifted evangelists who have the courage to ask this question.

But whom do we challenge first? In any strategy of evangelism, there have to be priorities. The Church Army, for example, has five priorities: older people, area evangelism, church planting, children and young people, and the homeless. I will highlight three crucial priority areas for 'The Conversion of England' in 2005.

Evangelism Among Children

We continue to reap the reward of serious and increasing neglect. What can we do to address this situation?

The Church of England's Children's Strategy outlines four key areas:

a   Worship and nurture of children
b   Children and evangelism
c   Supporting ministry among children
d   Training for ministry among children

This strategy needs all the support it can muster. We are in for the long haul and many of the key tasks and outcomes identified will take a considerable period of time to bear fruit. I would make a plea for urgency, with two particular pleas.

Firstly, that we agree that children should be the church's number one priority. According to George Barna, one of America's top researchers, 'If the Pastor/ Vicar does not include children as one of the top church priorities, the chance of that ministry reaching its potential and having a significant impact on the lives of the church's children is severely reduced.'[36] Bishop Gavin Reid has written, 'If we are to strengthen the memory of Christ in our society, where do we begin? We begin with children.' I agree with his convictions that, if we have the will and motivation for this, several things would follow:

- There would be stronger and more specifically Christian, youth work in our churches within ten years.
- There would be more young adults in our congregation in 15 to 20 years.
- There would be more younger candidates for ordained ministry.
- The Christian 'feel' to our society would increase rather than decrease.

It is right to invest in people when they are young. After all, it is well established that the religious beliefs a person develops by the age of 13 are pretty much the set of beliefs they will maintain until they die. We need to maximize the influence of the Christian story by investing in children.

Secondly, I think it is a splendid idea under the new Church of England strategy to develop a 'child-friendly award' for church. I want to raise the bar higher and ask for an award for transforming children into spiritual champions.

This means reaching children and growing them as disciples in a very intentional way. This nurturing is vital in the spiritual war going on for the minds, hearts and souls of our children. It is vital for strong, healthy foundations. And it can only be done in close partnership with parents. The church needs to equip parents strategically to help children develop spiritually. It needs to increase parents' confidence in their ability to raise spiritual champions. Surely it is possible to measure elements of transformation in children's lives. This might include breadth and depth of Bible knowledge, willingness to serve, involvement in worship, lifestyle and other evidence of growing in Christ-likeness.

The question remains as to whether we have the leaders who have a passion for this ministry and are willing to fight the tough battles in terms of allocating the church's resources, motivating people's involvement and maintaining a high standard of quality.

Prayer

A key text has to be 2 Chronicles 7.14: 'If my people, who are called by my name, will humble themselves and pray and seek my face and turn from their wicked ways, then will I hear from heaven and will forgive their sin and will heal their land.'

According to Selwyn Hughes, there are barriers that prevent the spiritual tide turning. Expounding the famous Chronicles verse he reminds us that:

- we are stuck in our pride;
- we do not pray enough, passionately enough;
- we are reluctant to turn from our wicked ways and genuinely repent.[37]

Interestingly, a new generation is learning to pray and to link that prayer with mission. The 24/7 prayer movement is at the centre of a prayer revival across the globe. This new movement has realized that the opportunities are no longer those of the great post-war stadium rallies, but rather those of the 'worldwide web, budget travel, the rise of tribalism and the postmodern desire for community, authentic spirituality and authentic justice.'[38]

24/7 has caught the imagination of a rising generation. It has brought prayer and ministry together and encouraged social involvement and spiritual intimacy. This movement has brought a cultural and creative revolution in the way we pray. Prayer rooms have been created in a variety of settings (my garage was co-opted at one stage). All the prayer rooms that are on the go at any given time are connected on the website, sharing answers to prayers, as well as heartfelt prayer requests. This renewal movement of prayer appears genuinely excited about praying in the middle of the night. It is part of a messy spirituality of prayer, creativity, mission, justice, pilgrimage and community. It even talks of a new monasticism.

24/7 has brought praye and ministry together and encouraged social involvement and spiritual intimacy

An Effective Evangelism Process Course

Growing churches invariably run an effective evangelism and discipleship course. *Evangelism—which way now?*—an evaluation of *Alpha, Emmaus,* Cell Church and other contemporary strategies for evangelism—is a very good guide for this.[39] *Alpha* is probably the most well known. Over 1.6 million people have done the course in the UK.

As a local church, we have reaped the rewards of the belief that going on a conference makes a difference, and the more closely we have followed the recipe the better our results have been. We have always used our own speakers and regret some earlier courses when we did not always have a meal. We have had courses for adults with special needs, for men, and for 18–30s, as well as using *Youth Alpha* for confirmation preparation. Having attended an *Alpha* Strategy Conference, I see no fall in the motivation and no suggestion that the UK market has been saturated. The vision to re-evangelize the UK and see the transformation of society is still driving the many supporters of *Alpha*. At the end of my recent study leave, my first evening engagement was an *Alpha* celebration meal at the end of another course. I heard four wonderful testimonies, including that of John, who later wrote for the church magazine:

Having attended an Alpha Strategy Conference, I see no suggestion that the UK market has been saturated

> I have been coming to church for over four years. I have been attending Sunday services but just felt I was going through the motions of worship and praise. I would leave church with a feeling of emptiness and I felt alone and unloved, because I could not find my relationship with God. But that all changed when I went on an *Alpha* course. The turning point for me was the Holy Spirit away day. I experienced the presence of the Holy Spirit for myself through prayer. I left there with the feeling of such love, peace and confidence in God which you could not surpass. I later read a book, *After Alpha*, by Michael Green.[40] In it was an extract which could have been directed at me. It said, 'It is OK living your life within the Christian picture frame but if you have not got the photograph of Jesus in the centre, you have not got the complete picture.' But through *Alpha* I know my picture is now complete.

Now those who criticize *Alpha*, its methodology or theology, or even both, have to come up with their own more effective ways of bringing people to faith in Christ. It is quite possible that questions about *Alpha* have been the impetus behind churches looking at *Alpha*-inspired alternatives such as *Emmaus, Credo,* the Y course, *Christianity Explored, Essence, Start,* Cell Church and G 12. From this explosion, there is on offer a variety of both tried and experimental routes into the heart of God. My plea is for each church to use at least one course and do it well.

My plea is for each church to use at least one course and do it well

6   Evangelism: Preparing for the Gospel

> It must be remembered that when exhortation and suggestion are at variance, suggestion always wins. Christians must take their part in re-creating a sound social and cultural life, and thereby healing the modern divided consciousness in which head and heart have become divorced and man's conscious purposes are no longer in harmony with the forces which give direction and tone to their emotional life.
>
> William Temple

Having encouraged some ideas for sowing the seed, TTCE steps back and focuses on preparing the soil. Most of the chapter centres on the media. This again is something we can do today, with new resources.

E-Church Response

Applications to join www.i-church.org, the Church of England's first internet parish, have been 'absolutely overwhelming' and have 'far exceeded expectations,' says the Revd Richard Thomas, the Diocese of Oxford's Director of Communications. Soldiers serving in Iraq, US Marines, people with disability who are unable to get to church, carers who cannot leave the home for long periods of time, and residents of mid-Australia are just some of the people who have signed up for membership.

At a recent Christian Resources Exhibition, a 3-D church service in cyberspace was launched. The church can take 25 people who can shout, talk or whisper to each other. They can enter the pulpit and preach if it is empty, kneel at the altar or visit the crypt to scrutinize the notice boards. 'To our generation has been entrusted a new sphere of communication,' said the Bishop of London, the Rt Revd Richard Chartres.

Already in place are online Bible studies (see one launched by Church Army at www.word-on-the-web.co.uk) where subscribers read a short, challenging Bible study, along with a prayer, delivered straight to their email inbox.

Online church may not be a substitute for the real thing, but it is surely another medium for spreading good news. Can you imagine St Paul pressing the send button? Perhaps all churches should have a website with a link to www.ReJesus.co.uk.

The Cinema

It is important for the church to have constructive engagement with the cinema, which has a new appeal to many. One of the most recent examples has been Mel Gibson's *The Passion of the Christ*. Interestingly, Protestants have embraced this Catholic vision of Christ, because they are just grateful for any serious film about Christ. It is not uncommon for faith and piety to be mocked. One church I visited had a step by step strategy that included showing a filmed interview with the director Mel Gibson, excellent publicity and a six-week series. 'We'll look at who Christ was, what he taught, and how he loved us.' They also had a discussion group designed for spiritual seekers (and sceptics) to look at tough questions about faith, this time with a focus on *The Passion*. Two churches in my deanery regularly show films. In one case, they invite a large family audience over the doorstep and it is a community occasion where good relationships are being forged. In the other, specific films are chosen and discussion follows on. You might find similar opportunities with *The Lion, The Witch and the Wardrobe* when released.

A book such as *Praying the Movies* by Edward McNulty[41] has been the basis of an evening preaching series in my home church. Small groups have also discussed particular films. Earlier I noted how people have stopped reflecting on the afterlife. I immediately think of a scene from *Forrest Gump*. Tom Hanks, (Forrest) is at the graveside of his late wife, Jenny. He is wondering, 'Do we just show up and float like a feather on the breeze? Is there no destiny? I do not know if we each have a destiny or if we're all just floating around accidental like on a breeze.'

As TTCE advocated, we cannot overestimate the power of film and TV, and particularly advertising, to shape our faith, values and behaviour. This is the place today for most people where what we value as human beings is revealed, along with our hopes and our fears. It asks our deepest questions, expresses our rage and reflects our most basic dreams. Too often, it shows bad news, which is only one side of the truth. Christians need to be there whenever possible saying, 'but there is good news, the bad news is not the only truth.'

Advertising

TTCE recognized the powers of press advertising and encouraged the church to make an adventure in Christian education through advertising on a nationwide scale. Obviously, a church on the margins does not have the finance to compete against some of the big corporations in the advertising field. However, we continue to see the advantage of advertising. The classic case is the *Alpha* course. It involves the country's biggest annual Christian advertising campaign. Billboards, bus panels and now taxis invite people to explore the meaning of life at a local *Alpha* course. The annual campaigns raise the profile of the course considerably. A Mori poll in October 2003 found that 20 per cent of the adult population of Great Britain, nearly 10 million people, now knows about *Alpha* and can identify it as a Christian course. The figure has gone up every September as a clear result of the poster and billboard initiative. In September 2000, just 9 per cent of British adults knew about *Alpha*. It is known that people are more likely to accept an invitation to an *Alpha* course if they have already heard of it.

If media visibility seems too difficult for the local church, what about advertising signs on church sites? Church notice boards are often in great need of improvement. Usually, they carry too much information; they are not always in the right position in relation to the traffic and too often are allowed to become worn and weather-beaten, communicating the sense that this might be a declining congregation. According to Kennon Callahan, 'Church signs should be two-or-three-second signs. That is, given the speed of the traffic that passes a church, there should be only as much information on the sign as a driver can read in 2 or 3 seconds. The 5 second sign has too much information on it. The driver will not read every part of such a sign.'[42]

If media visibility seems too difficult for the local church, what about advertising signs on church sites?

Many churches have not come to terms with the age of the car, either with signs or with car parking. Adequate signs that are at some angle to oncoming traffic will contribute to high visibility. It is interesting that there are plenty of firms offering good glass-fronted notice boards but not so many with creative colouring and positioning. As for car parking, are there any dioceses that have advisors for car parking and helpful ways of not annoying the neighbours? It is a shame when a church has worked hard on visibility and accessibility only to find that the attention of the community is caught by car parking problems. Although these factors are not as important as people who are visible in helping people, nevertheless they do contribute to our witness to the unbeliever.

Finally, in this section we have not mentioned literature and the use of screens, video projectors, and so on. My experience is that excellence honours God and inspires people. According to George MacDonald, 'The sight of such human excellence awakes a faint ideal of the divine perfection.' We need to invest in the best.

All this is still only preparing the soil but let us not underestimate the ways that contribute to and work against the reception of the gospel seed.

The Church: Christ's Weapon for Evangelism   7

> Christ wrote no book; he left in the world as his witness a 'body' of men and women upon whom the Spirit came. There was to be nothing stereotyped. The living society—the church—was to be the primary witness.   William Temple

According to *Evangelism—which way now?*, 'Non-Christians who are searching for spirituality today naturally turn to bookshops, evening classes and magazines rather than church.' We are also in an age where people hold back from active, open commitment.

But I do believe in the local church, as did TTCE. I even believe it has the capability of turning the tide of history, as Bill Hybels wrote: 'the local church is the hope of the world.'[43] My own church's mission is to pass on the baton of faith in Jesus Christ. And, in the area, our mission plan is entitled, 'Where churches resource one another and faith provokes faith.' I do not fully understand Paul's view of the church, in Ephesians 3.10, but it seems quite an amazing, cosmic task 'that through the church, the manifold wisdom of God might now be made known to the principalities and powers in the heavenly places.'

I believe that the local church has the capability of turning the tide of history

I was very involved in the Lent '86 study course, *What on earth is the church for?*[44] Over a million replies revealed a range of reasons why people go to church. I like Karl Barth's definition quoted in Philip Yancey's book, *Church: Why Bother?* 'The church exists to set up in the world a new sign which is radically dissimilar to the world's own manner and which contradicts it in a way which is full of promise.'

But why are people turning away from church? And what does 'church' mean in the setting of 'Fresh Expressions'? Yancey writes, 'Many churches offer more entertainment than worship, more uniformity than diversity, more exclusivity than outreach, more law than grace. Nothing troubles my faith more than my disappointment with the visible church.'[45]

As I write this, I have just been alerted to a lot of vandalism going on outside the church building next door to the vicarage. Paint is sprayed everywhere. They have even removed the grilles on the windows to spray them. Not so far away, a local church family has quarrelled. The churchwarden and treasurer have resigned. It will probably die down again just as quickly, in true Liverpool fashion, but it is the reality of church life. Where is the promise? Where is the big difference from the world?

I tend to think of the church a bit like our efforts at family prayers. When our three children were younger, we tried numerous ways of finding the best pattern for family devotions. My wife particularly encouraged us with different books and different ways of praying. For all sorts of reasons, I do not think we ever really cracked it. But we kept on trying.

I feel a bit like that with the church. We never reach the ideal but we have to keep trying—particularly in the following directions.

We never reach the ideal but we have to keep trying

To Meet with God

In my own parish, I have an 8 am Holy Communion (traditional), 9.30 am Holy Communion (modern/*Common Worship*), 11 am Family service and 6.30 pm Evening worship. The Communion services together attract between 60 and 80 people. The informal services attract between 300 and 400. What does that say?

Maybe we do not use the same flexibility and imagination in the more structured services. But people vote with their feet and I am amazed at how many parishes have bought and use *Common Worship* books. Working through this resource book does not seem to me to be attractive to nominal believers and seekers. And why do so many churches persist with the 'insider' service of Holy Communion as the main and sometimes the only service on offer? Gavin Reid says, 'That may be acceptable in a gathered church, but it is not acceptable in a church claiming to be the inclusive church that serves England.'[46]

On my study leave, I attended a lot of different worship services. Apart from a college chapel, the smallest gathering was 17 and the largest was a full auditorium of 4,000. The key element for me was expectation. No matter where I was, I had this confidence and expectancy that God had something to show me or something to say for my project. I was not disappointed and that expectant feeling took my gaze from the 'trappings' of musical style and other externals. It was easier in some settings than in others. In one Midlands church, I was told not to take my car for fear of vandalism and wrap up warmly because it was always cold. My faith level was dropping but, praise God, I was lifted and warmed by the worship.

In the Lake District, with 16 other people, we had been going for one and a half hours when the leader of the service checked with us that it was OK to carry on. It had been such a blessing thus far that everyone said, 'Yes, carry on.' I now find the challenge of maintaining that expectancy for four services each

Sunday in the same church building and at other times in the week. I know that meeting with God puts all the externals into their proper place.

To Reach Out to Different Groups

I visited two churches in multi-racial areas and they could not have been more different in outlook. One, in North London, was such a vibrant mixture of a host of different ethnic groups. The church seemed to radiate a welcome and hospitality. There were lots of points of contact with the community and the church buildings were in constant use for groups of all ages. The mixture of Afro-Caribbean, Asian and Anglo-Saxon backgrounds made it feel like a touch of heaven. Apart from a commitment to Christ, people would probably have little in common. There were those who were becoming Christians from Muslim backgrounds. One Muslim father told the church leader about his son: 'My son was a dog, but your community has made him a man.'

Compare this with another church I visited further north, where, at the evening service, the leader spoke openly of her fear of Islam. Not surprisingly, this church has made few inroads into the local community among any different groups other than the white, mainly middle-class congregation. I saw how fear can stifle hospitality and make people anxious about others who are different. In these days of European expansion, as the host nation, the host church, we have some great opportunities to demonstrate gospel hospitality.

To Look Outward

Each summer, we run a programme called 'Youthserve.' Our teenagers meet at 8 am for breakfast, worship and teaching, then they go off doing a whole variety of projects. They paint school fences, tidy gardens, entertain at nursing homes, run play schemes, decorate houses, and so on. They love it. They are given the opportunity to give and to serve and they pay £10 for the privilege. It is the old truth of sharing love and being enriched in the process. Adults need the same opportunities and it is often harder for suburban churches to find outreach opportunities.

We perhaps need to encourage more links with inner city churches and with projects abroad. It never ceases to amaze me how much good can be accomplished by a congregation of ordinary people who band together to minister to the needs among them. I see a glimpse of this in our prison ministry and in our service to those with special needs.

To Demonstrate Grace

My 84-year-old mother shops at Tesco's in Runcorn shopping city. When my father was ill, a till operator called Anne sent a card to my dad. When he became very ill, Anne visited him in hospital before he died. She knew him only from conversations in the supermarket at the check-out desk. Every week until Anne retired, we had to make sure we waited in Anne's queue. Although Anne is long since gone from the shop, my mother will not shop anywhere else out of regard for her love and kindness.

A troubled teenager in the church had been giving the family with whom she was living a hard time. After yet another reconciliation, she wrote in a card, 'Why don't you hate me?' The answer is grace. I sometimes wonder why God does not hate me, knowing some of the pain I have caused him. Yet he remains passionately involved with me. And I reckon I have met most grace-filled, passionately involved people in local churches. We do not always get it right but we keep trying.

'Why don't you hate me?'
The answer is grace

8 Conclusion

> Remember, the supreme wonder of the history of the Christian church is that always in moments when it has seemed most dead, out of its own body there has sprung up new life; so that in age after age it has renewed itself, and age after age by its renewal has carried the world forward into new stages of progress, as it will do for us in our day, if only we give ourselves in devotion to its Lord and take our place in its service.   William Temple

If we accept the argument that the nation's core religious culture has died, we have to understand why. Maybe we needed to die. Our effortless superiority as a church has been found wanting. We have fallen and declined. We have accelerated the disappearance of hope.

After the Roman ways had prevailed at the Synod of Whitby, the Celts did not give up. They went back to Lindisfarne and continued their mission with humility and grace. Is there not a lesson for us? The Church of England needs a resurrection, a dying to self and a rising from our failings, a new humility and grace, a sense of powerlessness apart from Christ, the head of the church. Our clergy need to die as religious functionaries and rise again as courageous leaders full of the grace of discretion. We need to be like Peter after Pentecost and not before. Our role on the margins of society means that we must eschew individualism and form partnerships that will help towards the conversion of England.

Notes

1   Report of a Commission on Evangelism appointed by the Archbishops of Canterbury and York, *Towards the Conversion of England* (London: Church Assembly, 1945).
2   J Sachs, *The Times*, 10th January 2004.
3   Lesslie Newbigin, *Foolishness to the Greeks* (Grand Rapids: Eerdmans, 1986) p 20.
4   *The UK Christian Handbook: Religious Trends 4* (London: Christian Research, 2004).
5   Frank Field, *Neighbours from Hell. The Politic of Behaviour* (Politico's Publishing, 2004).
6   George MacDonald, *The Princess and Curdie* (London: JM Dent & Sons Ltd, 1949) p 66.
7   Callum Brown, *The Death of Christian Britain* (London: Routledge, 2001).
8   Penny Thompson, *Whatever Happened to Religious Education?* (Cambridge: Lutterworth Press, 2004).
9   Interview with John Lennon: England, March 1966, quoted in USA August 1966.
10 Lesslie Newbigin, *The Other Side of 1984* (Geneva: World Council of Churches, 1983).
11 A report from the General Synod Board of Education and Board of Mission, *All God's Children? — Children's Evangelism Crisis* (London: National Society/Church House Publishing, 1991).
12 Geoff Pearson, *Save Our Children — A Personal Response to 'All God's Children?'* (Grove Evangelism booklet, Ev 23).
13 Penny Frank and Geoff Pearson, *Too Little — Too Late! Children's Evangelism Beyond Crisis* (Grove Evangelism booklet, Ev 41).
14 Philip Clark and Geoff Pearson, *Kidz Klubs — The Alpha of Children's Evangelism?* (Grove Evangelism booklet Ev 45).
15 Report by the Archbishop's Council, *Sharing the Good News with Children: The Church of England's Children's Strategy* (London: Church House Publishing, 2003).
16 Bob Jackson, *Hope for the Church* (London: Church House Publishing, 2002).
17 Ian Maher, *Faith and Film — Close Encounters of an Evangelistic Kind* (Grove Evangelism booklet, Ev 59).

18 Vernon Blackmore, *Using Your Church Web Site for Evangelism* (Grove Evangelism booklet, Ev 53).

19 www.christianity.org.uk

20 www.rejesus.co.uk

21 Bel Mooney, *Devout Sceptics* (London: Hodder & Stoughton, 2003).

22 Craig Bartholomew and Thorsten Moritz (eds), *Christ and Consumerism* (Cumbria: Paternoster Press, 2000) p 115.

23 A report from the Mission and Public Affairs Council, *Mission-Shaped Church* (London: Church House Publishing, 2004).

24 www.freshexpressions.org.uk

25 Donald English, *An Evangelical Theology of Preaching* (Nashville: Abingdon Press, 1996).

26 B P Stone, *Faith and Film* (St Louis, MO: Chalice Press, 2000).

27 John Finney, *Finding Faith Today* (London: Bible Society, 1992).

28 *The Ruin of Anglicans*, the results of a survey carried out by Christian Research in 2002

29 M Mittelberg, L Strobel and B Hybels, *Becoming a Contagious Christian* (Grand Rapids: Zondervan, 1995).

30 Bill Hybels, *Courageous Leadership* (Grand Rapids: Zondervan, 2002).

31 *Lost for Words* (CPAS, 2002).

32 *Gossiping the Gospel*—Evangelism Course from the Uniting Church in Australia, 1992.

33 Through Faith Missions, 73 High St, Coton, Cambridge, CB3 7PL.

34 Mark Greene, *Imagine* (London Institute for Contemporary Christianity, 2003)

35 Michael Green, *Evangelism in the Early Church* (London: Hodder & Stoughton, 1970).

36 George Barna, *Transforming Children into Spiritual Champions* (California: Regal Books, 2003); Gavin Reid, *To Canterbury with Love* (Eastbourne: Kingsway Communications Ltd, 2002).

37 Selwyn Hughes, *Why Revival Waits* (Farnham: CWR, 2003).

38 Peter Grieg, *Red Moon Rising* (Eastbourne: Kingsway Publications, 2004).

39 Mike Booker and Mark Ireland, *Evangelism—which way now?* (London: Church House Publishing, 2003).

40 Michael Green, *After Alpha* (Eastbourne: Kingsway Publications, 1998).

41 Edward McNulty, *Praying the Movies* (Louisville: Geneva Press, 2001).

42 Kennon Callahan, *Twelve Keys to an Effective Church* (San Francisco: Harper and Row, 1983).

43 Bill Hybels, *Courageous Leadership* (Grand Rapids: Zondervan, 2002) p 15.

44 Martin Reardon, *What on Earth is the Church for?* (London: British Council of Churches and The Catholic Truth Society, 1985).

45 Philip Yancey, *Church: Why Bother?* (Grand Rapids: Zondervan, 1998).

46 Gavin Reid, *To Canterbury With Love* (Eastbourne: Kingsway Publications, 2002).